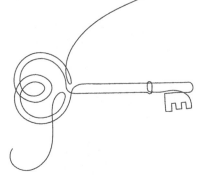

Finding Me

k. buehler

Finding Me
copyright © 2025 by k. buehler
All rights reserved.

No part of this book may be used or reproduced in any manner whatsoever without written permission except in the case of reprints in the context of reviews.

Printed in the United States of America
Published by NOW LLC

ISBN: 979-8-9907284-3-1 (trade paperback)

Dedication

To all the mirrors—
the people who held my gaze,
even when it trembled,
and the moments that shattered me,
only to show me the pieces
I didn't know I needed to find.

To the voices that whispered truths
I wasn't ready to hear,
and the silences that taught me
how to listen to my own.

To the love that expanded me,
the pain that reshaped me,
and the hope that kept me moving forward
when the road was too dark to see.

To every reflection—
soft or jagged,
kind or unyielding—
that dared me to face myself
and reminded me
that I am whole,
even in my breaking.
This is for you.

Acknowledgements

To my daughter, Amelia Ann—your brilliance, curiosity, and love remind me daily of the beauty of being fully seen and fully known. You inspire me to show up as my most authentic self, and because of you, I will always find my way back home to who I am.

To my partner, Aaron—who holds space for my process and encourages me to embrace joy, thank you for your unwavering presence and support.

To the Buehler writers, poets, and creatives whose blood and ink flow through my veins—I honor you. These poems are a continuation of a legacy I once didn't know I carried, and now step into with pride.

To those who have walked with me in the darkest valleys and celebrated with me on the mountaintops—your love, understanding, and belief in me have been my compass. To the friends who reminded me I was never truly alone, and to the mentors who saw the light in me even when I couldn't, I am forever grateful.

To the soul reading this—thank you for holding these words, for seeing me, and, in turn, allowing yourselves to be seen. May you find pieces of yourself within these pages, and may you, too, step into the fullness of who you are.

And finally, to the girl I used to be—the one who thought she had to shrink, silence herself, or become someone else to be loved—this is for you. You were always enough. You are found. You are free.

Foreword

Some voices are whispered, some are sung, and some—like the one in this book—create intricate etchings on your soul.

I have had the profound privilege of knowing the poet behind these words for over a decade. She is more than a friend; she is a force, a light, a testament to resilience and beauty despite the shadows and slicings of trauma she has endured, overcome.

Through the years, I have been honored to serve as her mentor, her sounding board, her steadfast encourager. The truth, however, is that she has taught me so much more than I have taught her - about courage, about survival, about the sheer power of twisting pain into poetry. Every verse in this collection reflects the places, pieces and pits of her journey, woven with wisdom, raw emotion, and an honesty that is both breathtaking and necessary.

Her words are not just poetry; they are literary art. They move me, stir me, remind me why I fell in love with language in the first place. And I have no doubt they will move you, too. This book is more than a collection of poems; it is a reckoning, a revelation, a radiant offering from a soul who has walked through fire and emerged stronger, shining a bright, hot, vital light.

foreword

As you turn these pages, soak up each word. Let them wash over you and infiltrate your inner artist, adding to the animation of your soul. Prepare to be captivated. Prepare to feel deeply. Prepare to witness a heart that refuses to be anything less than luminous.

With admiration and love,
Rachelle K. Keck, PhD, JD

Note From The Poet

I have always found comfort in words. Even before I understood their power, I knew they could hold things too heavy to carry alone—grief, love, questions, truth. Writing has always been how I make sense of the world, how I untangle what's inside me and lay it down in a way that feels real.

Finding Me is a collection of those moments—of sitting with what aches, of letting go, of finding beauty in what once felt broken. These poems were not written with the intent to be perfect; they were written because they needed to exist. They are remnants of healing, markers of where I have been, and invitations to reflect on where we are all going.

This book is for anyone who has ever felt lost, unseen, or unsure of where they belong. For those who have held questions bigger than answers, and for those who have had to piece themselves back together after loss, change, or simply the weight of being human. These words are not about arriving at certainty, they are about honoring the journey—about finding yourself, over and over again, in the spaces between what was and what could be.

If there is even one line that resonates, one verse that reminds you of your own strength, or one moment where you feel a little less alone, then these words have done what they were meant to do. They found you.

With love,
k. buehler

Chapters

Discovery	0
Healing	12
Connection	23
Faith	36
Liberation	51
Growth	75
Resilience	73
Hope	85
Joy	91

Discovery

You are not lost; you are hidden beneath the layers you once thought were yourself.

Curious You

You are an echo of what has been forgotten—
the wisdom of wonder,
the freedom of love,
the audacity of dreaming.

How do we remember
what it means to know ourselves?
Not the self they sell to us,
the self that burns
with ancient truths,
the self that becomes whole
as it breaks.

What if curiosity was a birthright,
where knowing yourself
was a revolution?
Where loving your neighbor
is not just a command,
it is a way of being?

What if curiosity is a mirror,
reflecting the question:
Who am I becoming and
how does my light
spark the light in others?

The Echo

I met myself for the first time
when I peeled away the masks,
layer by layer,
until I was naked
and afraid to look.

The reflection was not kind.
It showed me the scars I had hidden,
the lies I had believed,
the stories I had told to survive.

Yet as I stood there,
quivering beneath the weight of truth,
I felt a pulse—
a rhythm deep in my chest,
an echo of a self
I had long forgotten.

Metaphors

I found myself
between the metaphors,
in the spaces where words
refuse to lie.
The pen didn't shy away
from the truth.
It bled the reality
I was too afraid to speak.

In similes,
I became like the ocean—
vast, uncontainable,
filled with waves that crash
and then recede.

In metaphors,
I became the phoenix—
rising from ashes I didn't know
could still burn.
Poetry gave me permission
to be everything I thought
I wasn't allowed to be.

Gift
The pen became a gift
I gave to myself.
Not to impress,
not to perform,
to heal.

It held my truths
when I couldn't speak them.
It carried my grief
when it felt too heavy to hold.
And in its quiet power,
it reminded me
that my story is mine to tell.

Healing isn't about erasing the past.
It's about finding the beauty
in the telling.

Alchemy
Words turned my wounds
into wisdom.
Every syllable,
a salve for the places
that ached.

I spilled my grief
onto paper
and watched it transform
into something golden,
something alive.

Through poetry,
I found that healing
isn't erasure.
It's alchemy.
It's turning pain
into power,
turning loss
into light.

Looking Glass
In the act of writing,
I stopped running.
I stood still
and faced myself.
The paper held my truth
when my heart couldn't.
And through its reflection,
I began to see myself clearly—
not perfect,
but whole.

Falling Into Me
I spent years
trying to hold up the world,
shoving myself aside
to make space for everyone else.

Now, I let go.
I fall, not into emptiness,
into myself—
a soft place
I'd forgotten how to land.

Untamed
They tried to tell me
what a good life looks like—
contained, controlled, predictable.

Yet my life is untamed.
It spills over boundaries,
lights up dark spaces.

I don't want their version of good.
I want my wild, authentic experience.

Becoming

I wrote to understand,
but in the process,
I became.
The poet in me
was always there,
waiting to take my hand
and lead me back
to myself.

Through every verse,
I found pieces of a puzzle
I didn't know I was solving.
Each poem,
a map of my becoming.

I am not just the poet.
I am the poem.

Dialogue

Poetry wasn't just words on a page.
It was a conversation—
me, speaking to myself.

I asked,
"What are you afraid of?"
And the poem answered,
"Not being enough."

I whispered,
"What do you need?"
And the poem replied,
"To be seen, to be loved,
to feel safe in your own skin."

Through every question,
every answer,
I found pieces of myself
I had long forgotten.
Poetry gave me back
to me.

Priority

Most of my life,
I've felt like an inconvenient option.
When my mother chose to stay
with the man who forced my conception.
At six, when the state said
my parents didn't want me.
At seven, when the foster family
chose my brothers but not me.
At ten, when my adoptive mom
told me she wanted a baby instead.
At thirteen, when she said boys liked me
because I came from a whore.

At seventeen, when I found him
with my best friend.
At nineteen, when I met the soul
that awakened my desires.
At twenty-one, when we tried again,
and decided I wasn't the one.
At twenty-four, when I chose a man
who seemed like a safe choice.

And then at thirty-three,
I chose myself.
Not as an option,
as the priority.
Because life doesn't wait
for someone else to see your worth—
you must claim it.

The road to self-love is tangled,
and it's the only one that leads home.

Healing

Healing does not erase; it alchemizes.
Pain becomes the gold that lines the cracks.

Grief

I sat with my grief,
invited it to tea.
It showed me its face—
hollow eyes, trembling hands,
a mirror of my own reflection.

"What do you want from me?" I asked,
but it didn't answer.
It just sat there,
its silence heavier than words.

So I held it.
Let it seep into my skin,
fill the cracks I had plastered shut.

Meeting Me
I thought healing would feel
like conquering mountains,
like slaying the demons of my past.
But it felt more like sitting quietly
with my own reflection,
watching the walls I'd built
slowly crumble.

Healing showed me
how to meet myself again—
not the version others wanted,
but the me who had been waiting,
patient and gentle.
She wasn't perfect,
but she was worthy.
She wasn't fearless,
but she was whole.

Language of Healing
Healing speaks in metaphors.
It doesn't come as a clean answer,
but as an invitation
to explore.

Through poetry,
I learned to speak its language.
To let the rhymes guide me
to the places that hurt.
To let the rhythm
echo the heartbeat
I had ignored for so long.

Healing doesn't shout.
It whispers through the lines,
waiting for me to pause,
to listen,
to breathe.

Edits

The story they told me
was one of lack,
of always striving,
always falling short.

Then came the moment,
I picked up the pen.
I crossed out the lies:
"Not good enough.
Not deserving.
Not lovable."

And I wrote a new story:
I am worthy.
I am whole.
I am enough.
The act of writing became healing.
The act of believing became freedom.

Through Lines

Poetry became the thread
that stitched me back together.
Each word, a tiny stitch,
pulling the pieces of me
into something whole.

I poured my pain onto the page,
watching it transform—
from weight to wings,
from silence to song.
The lines didn't erase the hurt,
but they gave it meaning,
a place to rest
outside my chest.

In the rhythm of writing,
I met myself.
Not the version they wanted,
but the me who had always been waiting—
raw, wild, untamed.

Burn

The ashes of lies
covered me once,
a suffocating dust.

Yet my daughter's gaze
called me to rise,
to show her how
fire can purify
instead of destroying.

Now, I am not afraid to burn.

Weight

They told me I wasn't enough—
not holy enough,
not kind enough,
not deserving enough.
I carried that lie
like a stone in my chest,
heavy and unrelenting.

But in the quiet of solitude,
I learned to ask the question:
Who told you this?
And I saw their faces,
heard their voices,
felt the shame they passed down,
generation after generation.

That stone was never mine to carry.
I placed it down
and found, in its absence,
a weightlessness
I didn't know I could feel.

The Body Speaks
The body remembers
what the mind tries to forget.
The tension in my shoulders,
the ache in my chest—
they're not just pain;
they're messages.

Healing taught me to listen:
To the way my breath shortens
when fear whispers.
To the way my heart races
when I feel unseen.
The body doesn't lie;
it just waits for me to notice.

Healing is not about silence;
it's about translating
what my body already knows.

Acceptance
Healing isn't fixing;
it's accepting.
It's sitting with the parts of myself
I once tried to hide
and saying,
"You're welcome here."

It's letting go of the war within,
the constant battle for perfection.
It's finding peace
in the messy, beautiful truth
of being human.

Acceptance isn't passive;
it's powerful.
It's the light that shines
even in the darkest corners.

Presence

Sit with your pain,
as you would a friend.
Ask it why it's here,
what it needs,
what it's trying to teach you.

In counseling, they tell you:
"Name the feeling.
Hold it, don't fight it."
And so I hold anger,
shame,
grief.
I name them,
and in doing so,
I disarm them.

Healing is not the absence of struggle.
It's the presence of self.

Connection

Every soul you touch is a reflection of the one within you. Love them, and you love yourself.

Fingerprints

Every person I've ever loved
has left fingerprints on my soul.
Some pressed gently,
others left bruises,
but all of them shaped me.

I see their faces in the quiet moments—
a laugh, a song, a smell of rain.
They haunt me,
not with regret,
with the ache of what could have been.

And yet, it is their shadows
that teach me to love better,
to reach deeper,
to open wider.

Because love is never lost.
It just changes form.

Love Like Nature
Nature is the first lover,
always giving,
always offering lessons
if we're willing to listen.

The sunrise shows me resilience,
how light follows darkness
without fail.
The storm shows me release,
how to let go of the tension
so I can grow.

Love is not so different.
It is cyclical, infinite,
a wise teacher that whispers,
then roars.
It asks for patience
then rewards us with clarity.
It shows us that endings
are simply beginnings in disguise.

Just as the ocean never hoards its waves,
love doesn't cling;
it flows.
It transforms us,
wearing down our sharp edges
until we are smooth enough
to hold more.

Love, like nature,
teaches us that life is not linear.
It's a spiral of learning,
of giving and receiving,
of falling apart
and coming back together.

Love Brought Me Back
I thought love was about finding someone else,
but it brought me back to me.
Every embrace
showed me what I could give.
Every heartbreak
revealed what I could survive.

In love, I saw my reflection—
the cracks, the scars,
the light that spilled through anyway.

And like nature,
love reminded me
that nothing is wasted.
Even the pain
becomes part of the cycle,
a lesson planted deep,
ready to bloom
when the time is right.

Shadows

I chased the shadow of the trees,
calling it shelter,
but they called it shade.

How strange, I thought,
that they gave their darkness freely,
even as their roots anchored light.

I realized my shadow
wasn't my burden to bear,
it was the place where I could rest
and meet myself.

Not an absence of light,
rather the space where light
waits to return.

Facing Truth
Relationships are the purest classrooms,
where lessons don't come as lectures,
they teach us as reflections.
Every interaction a mirror,
showing us parts of ourselves
we didn't know existed.

In love, I see my softness,
the corners of my heart that crave connection.
In conflict, I meet my shadow,
the edges of my soul
that I've tried to hide.
The people who challenge me
don't break me;
they sharpen me.
They ask me to stretch,
to grow beyond my comfort,
to choose patience, forgiveness, and truth.

It is in relationships—
messy, raw, imperfect—
that I meet myself deeply.
I find the wounds I thought had healed,
the dreams I thought I'd lost,
the courage I didn't know I had.

And when someone else meets me,
truly sees me,
it reminds me to see myself.
Because love is a mirror, and in it,
we find the face of our truest self.

Reflection Pool

There's a pool in the woods,
still as glass,
deep as eternity.
When I look into it,
I see the faces of everyone
I've ever loved.

Each one taught me something—
patience, resilience, vulnerability.
Each one left ripples
that I carry to this day.

In that reflection,
I see myself too.
Not just who I am,
who I'm becoming.

Love isn't a destination.
It's a reflection pool,
showing me the depths
I have yet to explore.

Broken Prism

You shattered me
into fragments of light,
not emptiness.

I became sharp edges,
too jagged to hold.
Each shard caught the sun,
refracting my agony
into a kaleidoscope of meaning.

What broke me
also made me infinite,
an explosion of hues
born from multiple fractures.

Held, Not Healed
I thought healing meant mending,
but sometimes it's being held—
by the arms of a partner
who sees you even when you cannot.

Love didn't fix me;
it reminded me I am whole
just as I was and now as I am.

We Built This

Love isn't something we found.
It's something we built.

Brick by brick,
day by day,
we created a space
where love lives
without fear of collapse.

Honey

They told me
healing takes time,
but what they didn't say
is it also takes sweetness.

My partner's kindness
is the honey that seeps
into the raw places of me.
Together, we turn scars
into gardens.

Kaleidoscope

I thought love was two colors—
black and white,
all or nothing.

Yet in this life,
I've discovered the spectrum.
With my partner,
and my child,
I live in hues
I never imagined existed.

Together, we are a kaleidoscope,
turning endlessly
toward the light.

Safe Space
True love is not perfect.
It's a place to rest,
to be messy,
to be whole.

Healing taught me to ask,
"What does safety feel like?"
I didn't know at first.
But then I remembered:
It feels like love that doesn't demand.
It feels like silence
that isn't uncomfortable.

Love isn't the absence of flaws.
It's the willingness to sit with them,
to say, "I see you,
and I choose you anyway."

Faith

Faith coexists with doubt; it is the courage to walk into the unknown with hope.

The Prayer I Didn't Ask For

You bow your head,
whispering petitions like raindrops
against a storm,
your words rising to the heavens
on my behalf,
woven with concern,
disgust, or dismay—
a language of salvation offered
where you see shadows.

You kneel,
not where I have stumbled,
but where you believe I've fallen,
your prayers cradling not my bruises
but your discomfort,
lifting what you call vulgarity
as if it were a weight
I asked you to bear.

To you, I offer no defense,
only the understanding
that art unsettles,
truth divides, and words—
raw and naked—
are rarely polite guests.

Know this, I do not need your prayers,
but I see the heart behind them—
a faith trying to make sense
of what refuses to fit into its frame.
Let your words fly if they must,
and know my own will remain.

For I have not fallen;
I have risen, with ink-stained hands
and a voice that will not bend
for approval of men.
When I prayed, God told me to write.

Revealed

I walked away from the altar
with empty hands.
The God they preached
was not the God I knew—
wild, untamed,
whispering through the wind.

I found divinity
in the curve of a river,
the stretch of the stars,
the rhythm of my own breath.

Faith is not a chain.
It is a fire—
untamed,
unrelenting,
burning away the lies
to reveal the truth within.

Reflections of Heaven

How could we ever find heaven within,
When taught our beginning was wrapped in sin?
Born from fire, forged in death's embrace,
Told we were broken, fallen from grace.

We are but mirrors of beliefs we hold,
Crafted by moments, both tender and bold.
Each experiment, each resonance of pain,
Etches a mark, a soul to sustain.

A trigger strikes, a forgotten chord,
A wound reopens, a memory stored.
Our bodies remember though our minds forget,
Reacting to shadows of time's silhouette.

But here in the chaos, a truth unfolds,
A chance to learn as our story is told.
To study our thoughts, our feelings, our fight,
To sit with the dark and uncover the light.

For in presence, the gift of life appears,
The shedding of masks, the quiet of fears.
Each wound a doorway, each note a key,
Unlocking the soul we were destined to be.

Liberating the paradigms of old,
Tearing the veil, the blindfold's hold.
Seeking truth where lies had reigned,
Breaking free from the chains ingrained.

We are vessels, filled with the stream,
A life force flowing, both subtle and unseen.
Energy courses, past and present collide,
Illuminating the depths we hide.

Our cups overflow, yet feel so dry,
As the unseen becomes seen, we wonder why.
Words and actions, the sparks of our core,
Reflections of heaven we've longed to explore.

Pupil and portal, wound and womb,
Black holes of pain, yet gardens in bloom.
Possibility dances with potential's flame,
In the ashes of sin, heaven whispers our name.

Salvation of Fear

They called it love,
but put me behind bars.
They called it grace,
but grace doesn't choke.
The church that raised me
taught me shame,
a gospel of fear disguised as salvation.

Questions were sins.
Doubt was rebellion.
And every time I tried to spread my wings,
they clipped them,
whispering,
"This is for your own good."

Love doesn't cage.
Love doesn't silence.
And I realized,
the God they preached
wasn't the one my soul knew.

Unlearning the lies
felt like peeling away layers of skin,
raw and exposed.
But underneath,
I found something whole.
I wasn't broken.
I was buried.

Love Without Fear

Their love was conditional.
"Follow the rules,
and you'll belong."
But love shouldn't hurt.
Love shouldn't shame.

I found a love outside their walls
that didn't ask me to shrink.
It let me expand,
to take up space,
to be fully, unapologetically me.

This love didn't look like theirs.
It wasn't tied to doctrines or dogma.
It was alive,
flowing through the earth,
the sky,
my soul.

The Fire That Never Asked to Burn

This is not a crisis,
it is a slow extinguishing,
a smothering of dreams
before they are embers.
We ask youth why their hearts
ache to break free,
as if the wind has not been strangled
before it could breathe.

We write the obituary of a generation
with every system that cages them,
every rule that demands silence
instead of curiosity.
The earth itself mourns,
knowing its future builders
are being taught to break.

This is a fire that never asked to burn—
a quiet revolution in every heart
that refuses to lose its soul to ash.

Chain on Fire
Fear was the chain they used
to hold me in place.
Fear of hell.
Fear of questions.
Fear of myself.

But fear can't hold what has
already burned.
I set the chain on fire
with every truth I learned,
with every step I took into the
unknown.

The ashes didn't scare me.
They reminded me
of the light in my soul.

Ocean Depths

The ocean doesn't apologize
for its depth.
It doesn't hide its waves
or silence its roar.
It simply is.

And in its vastness,
I see my own.
The parts of me
that feel too much,
that want too much,
are the same parts
that make me whole.

Love is like the ocean—
sometimes calm,
sometimes fierce,
always full.
It teaches me
that my depth is not a flaw;
it's my strength.

Gospel Truth

The gospel they preached
was one of control,
of submission dressed as devotion.
But I found a new gospel,
written in the stars
and whispered by the waves.

It said:
"You are enough.
You have always been enough."

It didn't demand my silence.
It didn't shame my questions.
It celebrated my voice,
my curiosity,
my search for truth.

This gospel didn't chain me;
it freed me.

Unboxed

They shamed me for asking,
as if curiosity was a curse.
Yet I've discovered
that questions are holy.

The Spirit meets me in the asking,
in the wondering,
in the refusal to settle for easy answers.
What if the kingdom of heaven
isn't a place,
but a state of becoming?
What if God is bigger
than the stories they told?
What if I was never meant
to fit into their box?

Questions didn't lead me away from faith.
They led me to freedom.

The Kingdom Within
How could they tell me heaven
was so far away?
When I found it in the stillness of rain?
When I felt it in the pulse of the ocean's tide?
When I saw it in the pupil of my own eye?

Heaven wasn't above me.
it wasn't below me.
It was inside me.

And yet, every moment outside myself
led me closer to it.
The sky, the stars, the soil,
all reflections of a truth
I had always carried.

Faith

Faith wasn't the absence of doubt.
It was the willingness to step forward
even when I didn't know the way.

I found faith in the constancy of the seasons,
in the patience of seeds waiting to bloom.
I found faith in the way
the universe kept expanding,
never questioning its right to grow.

Faith wasn't something they could give me.
It was something I had to find
on my own.

Wild

They painted God
as a figure bound by rules,
sitting on a throne,
watching, judging.

Yet I met God in the woods,
barefoot on the moss,
branches tangled in the sky.
I met God in the laughter
of a friend who saw me.
I met God in the way
the tide kissed the shore,
again and again,
never giving up.

This God didn't fit
in their books or their rituals.
This God was alive,
as wild and untamed as me.

Lightning Thread

I followed the thread of lightning,
from the atmosphere to the earth.
It wove stories in the fabric of the sky,
that felt like they spoke to me.

Charged particles sang my name,
ions whispered:
You are not here by accident.
You are part of this circuit.

The sparks reminded me
that creation isn't quiet—
it's loud, it's chaotic,
it's brilliant.

And we carry that brilliance,
even in the moments we feel empty.

Liberation

Freedom is not given; it is claimed by those who refuse to be caged by the expectations of others.

Unlearning Silence

The first lesson they taught me
was to keep my voice small.
Don't ask too much.
Don't know too much.
Don't dream too big.

But the stars don't whisper;
they roar.
The ocean doesn't shrink;
it surges.
And I am not small.

Now my daughter watches.
So I unlearn silence
by listening to the wind.
It shows me that my voice
is part of the symphony.

Choose
Liberation is not a battle cry.
It is a quiet revolution—
the moment you choose yourself
over their expectations,
the moment you realize
you are enough.

Compass

Counseling isn't a cure;
it's a compass.
It doesn't give answers;
it gives me the courage
to find them myself.

In the quiet of the session,
I met myself.
The me I had silenced,
the me I had forgotten.
And I realized:
healing isn't becoming someone new.
It's returning to who I've always been.

The counselor said,
"Be gentle with yourself."
And so I was.
And in that gentleness,
I found the beginning of love.

Mirrors

Healing begins when I stop looking outward
and dare to meet my reflection.
Every relationship, every hurt,
a mirror that shows me the cracks I tried to hide.
But cracks don't mean brokenness;
they mean light is getting in.

What if every wound is a doorway?
A chance to step inside myself,
to tend the garden I've neglected.
Healing isn't fixing;
it's feeling.
It's allowing the hurt to speak
and listening with compassion.

Undoing

Undoing isn't a collapse.
It's the slow, deliberate removal
of what no longer fits.

I pull apart the lies, the roles,
the shame stitched into my skin.

I am threadbare,
I am not undone.

Unscripted
Once, I played the role they wrote for me
-obedient daughter, perfect mother, loving wife.

Now, I toss the script aside.
I am the author.
I am the artist.
I write messy, paint splattered stories
where my mistakes belong in the plot
and my truth is the climax.

Intimacy

I was taught there was a "right" way—
A way that saved me from myself,
That chained my body to a promise,
A vow that could only unlock love.

The "wrong" way carried weight,
A silent threat of God's wrath,
Of punishment,
Of shame carved deep into my skin.

For those whose innocence was stolen,
A gray space hovered—
A fragile exception
For a broken child,
But never a reprieve.

I swallowed their lessons whole,
Believed their fear was love.
I taught it too,
Handing others the same script
That would one day break me.

The "right" way told me to wait—
To give my heart, my soul, my mind,
To lay bare my fears,
Confess my dreams,
Expose every corner of my being
Except my body.

I believed the lie
That attraction was dangerous,
That passion was sin,
That desire was a betrayal of God's design.
They said it would ruin me,
But I was already ruined.
My innocence was torn apart
Before I could even spell the word.

I was told my choices defined me—
That my worth could be measured
In the space between my legs.
I waited,
Not out of faith,
But out of fear.
....

Marriage didn't redeem me.
It made intimacy a duty,
A role to perform,
A contract sealed by submission.
To be a wife meant saying "yes"
Even when my heart screamed "no."

I see now how deeply I believed,
How I became both the prisoner
And the guard.
I thought I was protecting myself,
But I was only caging
Everything I was meant to be.

Desire is not sin.
Passion is not shame.
The body is not a battlefield
For purity's war.

Now I reclaim what was taken.
I gather the pieces of myself—
The broken, the beautiful, the whole.
I write a new story,
With ink drawn from raw truth.
Love, intimacy, and choice
Are mine to hold,
Mine to give,
Mine to live.

Every Shade
I am not just the light.
I am the shadows,
the in-between places,
the spaces where love and rage collide.

I don't have to choose one part.
I am every shade of me,
and that is enough.

Edges of My Soul
I am the captain of this ship,
The master of the waves I flip.
The storm bows not to my control,
it shapes the edges of my soul.

Clear is not the absence of hue,
it's the vision of life, raw and true.
A colorless fire, a prism refract,
the universe whispers: take your power back.
So here I stand, the vessel, the whole,
transmitting the frequency of my soul.

Clear

They argue that clear is not a color.
Not red, blue, green—no spectrum sheen.
I say, clear is the space between,
the vessel for light, the path unseen.
A windowpane, the wind of pain,
transparency where truth is gained.

We are scalar grids, stitched by sound,
each note, a ripple, a wave profound.
Our eyes, the pupils, black holes of sight,
transmitting the soul's deepest light.
The storm doesn't cage—it builds, it breaks,
repairing the heart for new shapes it makes.

Clear is the key to what we feel,
the doorway to what's hidden, real.
Like plasma, like copper, like air in the lungs,
it hums the truth on invisible tongues.
Clear isn't absence; it's everything—whole,
a mirror reflecting the shape of the soul.

Beyond The Veil
We were taught of sin, of hell, of loss,
But what if the veil was torn for us?
Not to bind, but to break the chain,
To show the truth behind the pain.
Look back to heal, to thank the tears,
For diamonds are born from buried years.

We are wombiverse, woven whole,
Portals of magic, gateways of soul.
Honor the shadow, for it holds the key,
To leap beyond the veil and see.
We are not memories, we are the dream,
Clear, vast, the light unseen.

Growth

The seed does not question the soil. It grows because it trusts the darkness to bring the light.

Forest Within

I walked into the forest
to escape,
and found myself instead.

Each tree stood as a reminder:
There is no rush to grow.
There is no shame in standing still.
There is no weakness in reaching
for the light.

Love is like the forest—
dense, layered,
a place where shadows and light
coexist.
It's here, in this tangle,
that I learn who I am.

Seasons

Nature doesn't lecture;
it teaches by showing.
It's the rhythm of tides,
the cycle of seasons,
the sun that rises after the longest night.

The trees taught me
how to stand still and grow,
to root deeply
and still reach for the sky.
The rivers whispered
that movement is necessary,
even if the path isn't clear.

Love is like this—
a perpetual cycle of becoming.
It's the rain falling into the earth,
the earth giving life to seeds,
the seeds growing into forests
that shade and shelter the world.

Love asks us to give without keeping score,
to trust the flow,
to embrace the messy beauty of change.
It's a lesson in surrender—
not to lose ourselves,
an invitation to find ourselves
in the giving, in the growing,
in the rhythm of reciprocity.

And just as nature teaches patience,
love asks us to wait,
to tend the soil of our hearts,
to honor the process
of blooming in our own time.

Perpetual

Love is a teacher
that doesn't grade on a curve.
It asks me to show up,
to try,
to fail,
to try again.

Nature is the same—
unforgiving,
but endlessly giving.
The sun doesn't wait
for my gratitude;
it shines anyway.

Together, love and nature
teach me the same truth:
Life is a lesson,
not a test.
There is no right way to love,
only the courage
to keep learning.

Forest of Forgiveness

Forgiveness isn't about letting them off the hook;
it's about freeing myself
from the weight of what they did.

In the forest, I learned
how to forgive.
The trees let their leaves fall
without holding on.
The earth swallows decay,
turning it into new life.

Forgiveness doesn't erase the hurt,
it clears the path
so I can walk forward.
It reminds me
that healing is not about them;
it's about me.

Leap

She sacrificed certainty for adventure,
traded comfort for the danger of discovery.
She left the easy path
for the forest calling her name.
She chose to lose herself
to find who she was created to be.
She witnessed the wisdom of what was
and all she dreamed.
In the darkest moment,
she found her inner light.
Daring greatly, she leaped into the unknown.
As she jumped,
she remembered she could not fall.
She co-authored the story
already written on the walls.

Journey to Wholeness
As she looked at the past,
she witnessed the road
that she traveled.
Before her eyes
was not a straight line.
Her journey to wholeness
and loving herself
was tangled with
backward twists,
forward bends,
roundabouts,
detours, and
pit stops for reflection—
periods of rest and retreat.
When she doubts
her progress or potential,
she reminds herself
of her wisdom and experience,
and remembers:
Without each move she has made,
she wouldn't be who
and where she is today.
She is her greatest love story.

The Weaver

I was born in the rhythm of storm and calm,
a tide pulled by names, silence, and song.
Roots scattered and tangled sought solid ground,
looking for safety where none could be found.
Child of the wind that never stayed,
each move a fragment, a price I paid.
Words once elusive found their way,
through cracks of trauma to light of day.

A healer, a mother, a poet, a guide,
I walk where the broken and the whole collide.
I am a story untamed, a verse set free,
a bridge between what was and what could be.
Where systems failed, I stood to rebuild,
transforming hollow spaces into gardens filled.

Every tear that I shed watered a seed
of courage, of truth, of unheard need.
A torch for voices buried and suppressed,
together we find light, a path, and rest.

My journey bends inward still,
seeking to honor the quiet will—
to unmask my soul, to feel my core,
to be fully me—nothing less, nothing more.

This river runs deep, its current strong,
a testament to where I've belonged—
not just in places, but in the air,
in whispers of justice, in radical care.
Here I stand, both rooted and free,
a poem still writing its destiny.

I am the weaver of broken threads,
dreaming to life what once was dead.

Resonance
I tuned myself like an instrument,
adjusting each chord
to match the hum of the world around me.
The waves of sound—
laughter, grief, curiosity,
even silence—
told me who I was.

Did my vibration match my vision?
Was my frequency aligned?

I found the answer not in the question,
the truth was in the resonance.

Resilience

Storms do not destroy; they sculpt. Let the wind carve you into something unbreakable.

Lessons in Leaving
The leaves fall every year,
yet the trees never mourn.
They know the cycle.
They trust the process.

I want to be like the trees,
to release what is ready,
to trust that even in loss,
I am making space for something new.

Love taught me this, too.
That sometimes,
the letting go
is the most loving thing we can do.

Curiosity
Fear grips tightly,
While curiosity loosens the knot.
Fear says, "Brace yourself,
the worst is coming."
Curiosity whispers,
"What can this storm teach you?"

Ask yourself:
What strength does this storm reveal?
What wound does it want me to heal?
What part of me is it asking to grow?

Let curiosity be your compass.
Turn toward the questions
you've been too afraid to ask.
Let them show you
the path through the chaos.

Shoreline

Not every storm ends
with sunlight breaking through clouds.
Some storms leave us wrecked,
adrift on open water.

Yet even here,
you have power.
You can gather the driftwood,
build a new shore,
and rest until your strength returns.

The storm doesn't decide who you are.
You decide what rises from the wreckage.
You decide the shape of your healing,
the story your scars will tell.

Storms Speak

Breathe deeply,
feel the air thread its way
through the knots inside you.
Life moves quickly—
we leap from one storm to another,
never asking the wind its name.

Storms speak a language,
sometimes we forget how to listen.
Each gust whispers truths we avoid.
Each wave, a mirror,
revealing who we've been
and who we might become.

Ask yourself, softly:
What storm am I standing in now?
Let the answer rise like a tide.
Let it guide you, not drown you.

The "I" of the Storm

Picture yourself in the storm—
winds shrieking, waves clawing at you.
And yet, there is stillness.
The storm cannot find its way
to the center of you.

Here in the eye,
you are calm.
You are steady.
You are not the storm's prey;
you are its witness.

This is your truth:
you are both the storm
and the one who calms it.
You are the ocean's roar
and the quiet beneath its surface.

Take a breath,
and feel your center hold.

Weight of Water

The storms we carry are heavy.
Waves crash with the weight of injustice,
winds howl with the sound of loss.
Rain falls in sheets of self-doubt.

We try to weather them alone,
thinking survival means silence.
But storms are meant to be felt,
to seep into the cracks
so we can find where healing begins.

Close your eyes, and let the storm touch you.
Feel its weight shift—
it isn't crushing you;
it's carving you, shaping you,
preparing you to hold more
than you thought possible.

Art of Weathering
Storms will come—
of course they will.
This is the nature of life.
But you are not made to break.

You are the sculptor of your stillness,
the keeper of your calm.
Let the wind carve your edges
until they shine.
Let the rain soften the soil
so something new can grow.

Take a breath.
Feel the storm quiet inside you.
You are more than its chaos,
more than its noise.
You are its peace,
its quiet transformation.

Soft Sunlight
Joy isn't loud.
It's soft mornings,
one hand resting on my back
while another flips pancakes.

It's the sound of my child
singing made-up songs,
off-key and unrestrained.

Joy is yellow—
not a flash of lightning,
more like soft sunlight
lingering in open spaces.

Red Reclaimed
Red was anger once.
Now it's life—
the rush of my heart
when my child says "I love you,"
the heat of a hand
wrapped around mine.

Red was fire once.
Now it's warmth.

Whispering Waves

Storms write stories on our skin.
Tales of betrayal, fear,
of trust broken like brittle branches.
We anchor ourselves to these narratives,
believing they are the only truth.

But what if we unmoored ourselves?
What if we let the storm
wash those stories clean?
What if, beneath the wreckage,
there was a new story waiting—
one of strength, of rising,
of finding the shore again?

Ask the waves:
What part of me is ready to let go?
What story am I ready to rewrite?

Then let them speak.

Hope

Hope is the rebellion of the soul against despair. It whispers, 'There is more.'

The Silence We Refuse to Keep
If the future is perishing,
then silence is complicity.
We do not whisper of hope;
we roar it into being.
We do not watch from the sidelines;
we stand in the storm.

Start with the heart.
Not because it is easy,
because it is the only place
that still knows how to beat
when systems try to crush it.

Healing is a defiance,
a declaration of existence
in a world that asks you to forget
who you are.
We will not forget.
We will illuminate
hearts and minds
until our flicker becomes a blaze
and the whole world remembers.

Inheritance

Regret left a bill
for my father,
for my mother,
for my father's father,
for my mother's mother.
for generation after generation,
Regret charged interest—
shame, abuse, and loss
storing up my family's wealth.

When regret came to me
and handed me the bill,
I reviewed each charge,
line by line.
my spirit almost broke.

My inheritance indebted me
to violence, hate, and despair—
a legacy marked by tragedy.
I searched for a silver spoon
but found only a bullet.
I heard the ghost of my potential
whispering through poverty.

Regret tried to take my agency.
it asked me to sign my name,
to seal the deal with despair,
but I had resolve.

Resiliency brokered a new contract.
I refused the inheritance of pain.
I began to collect a new currency,
exchanging history's debts
for something of my own making.

I opened my own bank.
each deposit was forged
from love, forgiveness, and hope—
a wealth my ancestors never knew.

Regret still tries to hand me the bill,
now I review it differently.
line by line,
I rewrite the charges,
and my spirit grows stronger.

This is my inheritance now:
an unyielding legacy of hope.

Future Worth Living For
What if you were not asked
to prove your pain
to earn your worth?
What if the only question was:
What do you dream of?

What if your world
was designed for you to thrive,
instead of survive?

This is not a fantasy.
This is the promise
we owe to the future.
A future where youth
do not wonder if life is worth living,
but know, with every breath,
that it is.

Because they helped build it.
Because they are seen.
Because they belong.

A future worth living for
is one worth fighting for.
And it begins with you.

Revolution in Bloom

When they tell you to shrink,
to bind yourself into their small boxes,
your answer is a song
they cannot silence.

The way you dream so loudly
they call it rebellion.
The way your laughter echoes
like a revolution in bloom.

It is the way
your heart still beats,
your mind still questions,
your spirit still dares
to imagine,
to dream,
to thrive,
to dare to be alive.

You are what's right with our world.
Remember this when they try
to tell you that you're wrong.

Not the End
When the young say,
"Is life worth living?"
it is not an end;
it is a question
meant to be answered
with action.

Tell them:
You are not wrong
for feeling the weight of the world.
You are not broken
for wanting more.
You are not small,
the systems that cage you
are collapsing under their own greed.

We are here to design
the future with you.
Not for you,
with you.
Because you are not just the future—
you are the present,
and the world needs you now.

Joy

Joy is not found in loudness; it is the quiet song of the soul remembering it is whole.

Shape of Peace
Peace.
It is not the absence of noise,
hush of the crowd,
or lull in the storm.
Peace is a rhythm,
the song we've forgotten,
the melody buried beneath
the static of survival.

Peace is not a gift
wrapped in gold.
It's a choice,
intentional surrender
and release of control.

I have known peace
in the silence of early mornings,
when the world is too sleepy
to be washed away by currents of chaos.
I have witnessed it—
in the way my daughter laughs,
unapologetic and full,
reminding me peace is not perfect
it's pure.

Peace is messy.
The courage to hold
your broken pieces,
admiring them,
with love and compassion.
It's not about fixing,
it's mending with gold,
scars that create a map
of where we've been,
not where we'll stay.

Peace speaks to the soul,
it whispers:
"You are enough."
Peace grows in the cracks
where the world sought to
destroy our hope,
and in the breaking
poured out our light.

It's the way we love,
not because it's easy,
because it's necessary.
It's the way we forgive,
not to forget,
to be free.

Peace is a revolution,
a soft rebellion
against fear,
against hate,
against the falsehood
that isolation makes us strong.

I speak for peace,
but not the kind we are sold.
Not the kind that silences truth
or hides behind walls.
I am speaking of peace that burns apathy,
that reminds us to hope,
that plants seeds
in the ashes.

Sometimes I stop and wonder,
are we peace makers?
Are we building peace,
with our hands,
with our words,
with our hearts,
Who will shape a world
where peace isn't a dream,
it's a way of being?

For Her
For my daughter,
I deconstruct the myths—
that love is earned,
that worth is given,
that beauty has borders.

I build her a world
where she knows
she is the center
of her own story.

Truth In Her Eyes
My daughter doesn't speak
of perfection.
She asks questions
about the sky,
the way it changes
without warning.

Her eyes hold
a truth I'd forgotten—
we don't have to make sense
to be beautiful.

Through the Window
I used to look at the world
through barred glass,
fogged with expectations.

Now, my window is clear.
I see trees bending with the wind,
sunlight shifting in endless patterns.
The world reminds me
it was never the bars—
just the stories I believed.

The Bridge
Transformation is the ultimate sacrifice.
One thing dies
so another can live.
Death becomes
a blanket of darkness—
pain we must feel,
sorrow we must shed,
an invitation to grieve.
The place where
silence is loud.
The space where
shadows become shade,
hurt touches healing,
lead turns to gold.
Darkness holds tension
between the familiar
and the unknown,
the bridge we cross
to find the promise.

About the Poet

k. tedrow is a poet, storyteller, and truth-seeker who writes from the raw spaces of healing, identity, and transformation. With words that cut deep and linger long after the page is turned, she explores the tension between breaking and becoming, between past wounds and the courage to rewrite one's own story.

Her work is rooted in lived experience—navigating grief, trauma, faith, and the ongoing journey of self-discovery. Through poetry, she unearths the quiet truths we often avoid, making space for reflection, reckoning, and release. Her writing is not about perfection but about presence—about showing up, feeling deeply, and choosing authenticity over approval.

Beyond poetry, k. tedrow is a fierce advocate for those often unheard, using her voice to amplify stories that challenge systems, spark change, and inspire radical belonging. Whether speaking, facilitating, or writing, her mission is the same: to create spaces where truth is honored, healing is possible, and people feel seen.

Her debut collection, Finding Me, is a deeply personal exploration of identity, faith, and resilience—an invitation for readers to embrace their own becoming.

Other Work by k. buehler

Shadows of Light
(Available on Amazon)

Made in the USA
Monee, IL
21 February 2025